A Disciplined Mind and a Plan to Achieve It

Paul Halpine

NEWMAN SPRINGS PUBLISHING
320 Broad Street
Red Bank, NJ 07701

First originally published by Newman Springs Publishing 2019

ISBN 978-1-64531-009-9 (Paperback)
ISBN 978-1-64531-010-5 (Digital)

Printed in the United States of America

Acknowledgments

It would be impossible to thank all of the students, athletes, fellow coaches, and teachers who have so greatly impacted my life. As I look back on my career, I am constantly reminded of how fortunate I have been to have had a career as a teacher, coach, and counselor. I would be extremely remiss however if I failed to mention my wife Sue who has been my best friend, inspiration, and role model throughout my career and life. I also want to thank my sons, Pat and Tim, who have been two of my biggest supporters and greatest joys of my life.

Introduction

As a retired high school counselor, teacher, and coach, with over thirty-five years of experience, I have developed a passionate interest in how our mind and thoughts influence who we are, how we act, and what we are able to accomplish. Much of my study has been devoted to successful coaches, businessmen and women, teachers, as well as religious leaders, military figures, and everyday people who have accomplished extraordinary things. These individuals give every impression of leading happy, fulfilling, and rewarding lives. I have devoured countless books on positive thinking, mental discipline, and the factors that lead people to success and happiness. I have spent as much time as possibly talking with successful, happy, well-adjusted people. I have been inspired by so much of what I have heard and read.

As I began my writing and preparing to transition from a high school counselor to becoming a life coach/counselor, I wondered what I might have to offer that had not been presented by individuals with far more impressive credentials and life experiences than myself. I began by exploring what I considered to be my strengths and what I might have to offer. I looked back on my former teachers, coaches, and mentors, people who I admired, and who had influenced me. Seven key factors about all these individuals stuck out in my mind.

1.   All my teachers, coaches, and mentors possessed great mental strength and discipline. None of these individuals were discouraged by life's inevitable challenges and setbacks. While I had witnessed several of these individuals experi-

ence disappointments, never was there any indication they would fold the tent and quit.

2. I also observed that these were people of great character. All of the individuals acted honorably and ethically, and they were more than willing to share their experiences and life lessons.

3. All of the these highly successful individuals had a very specific philosophy of life and work, and they trusted their philosophy. They also talked about trusting their instincts. I discovered that these instincts stemmed from their philosophy, and it was apparent that their philosophy was formulated through years of study and hard work.

4. Everyone I visited with discussed the need to act. Plan, think, organize, but at some point, we have to pull the trigger. There will never be a perfect time or situation for any new endeavor. There will always be concerns and challenges. Trust yourself and your system—commit and act.

5. It became apparent that these individuals could break down what seemed to me to be complex concepts and simplify them so that I could more easily grasp the information being presented. There is no question; it is possible to over simplify difficult and complex issues, but at the same time, there can be a tendency to over complicate issues and make things harder than they need to be. The philosophy of simplification tied into my own teaching ideology, that it is best to begin with basic easily understood concepts. From there, I could move forward. If, however, there are too many difficult concepts presented initially, confusion could set in, and as the instructor, I would have to go back and reteach. You can always add information and clarify, but when a person is overly confused, frustration sets in, and the learning process is delayed.

6. The other thing I recollected about my favorite teachers, mentors, and coaches was that, by and large, they were encouragers. They created in me a sense of confidence that I was as capable as anyone in achieving my goals. There

were times when their comments were direct and straightforward, but there was never any question that all correction was designed to help me achieve at my highest levels; it was never personal.

7. The final component that I felt might be helpful, and that my teachers and mentors provided me was a specific plan to help achieve my goals. I am confident that the plan is what will assist you as much as any of the information presented. As much as the philosophy and psychology are important, it is the plan that will help us to actually act and implement our newly gained knowledge. It is the plan that will help us make the desired changes in our life. It is important to know where we want to go, but knowing what to do in order to achieve our goal is the real key to making change.

> I am confident that the plan is what will assist you as much as any of the information presented.
> As much as the philosophy and psychology are important, it is the plan that will actually help us act.

I think it would be helpful to understand that, after considerable study, I have adopted a cognitive-behavioral philosophy of coaching/counseling. Simply stated cognitive-behaviorists believe that individuals can change their lives for the better by controlling their thoughts (cognitive) and actions (behavioral). In fact, the only things we truly control in life are our thoughts and actions. We can try and influence, persuade, coerce, threaten, bargain, teach, but the only things we really control are our own thoughts and actions. For some, the idea that we control our thoughts comes as a foreign concept. Many believe that thoughts simply appear, and we have no power but to submit to them. Likewise, these individuals are under the mistaken impression that our emotions and feelings pop out of nowhere. These individuals have not yet come to the realization that feelings and emotions are the result of our thoughts. Unfortunately for many, this is the path they choose. These are the unfortunate individuals who have not developed the mental strength and discipline necessary to control their thoughts. It is my suggestion that as we begin to make significant changes in our life, we start by disciplining our mind, controlling our thoughts and actions, and making certain these thoughts and actions are consistently calm, positive, constructive, and rational.

Much of what will be presented here is designed to assist in developing the mental capacity necessary to control our thoughts and resulting actions. Learning to control our thoughts and actions is a skill and like any other skill, can be developed with consistent practice. To be successful, we need to devote significant time, effort, and energy to this specific area. Let us first dispel the notion that individuals who have learned to control their thoughts and actions have been born with superior mental capacities. Mental strength and discipline are not traits bestowed upon a lucky few, nor do these people have fewer challenges or stress than the rest of us. Rather, these individuals have chosen a more useful and productive thought process. They have made a commitment to monitoring their thoughts and actions and making both calm, positive, constructive, and rational. These thoughts over time become habits and eventually a productive way of life. Individuals with weak undisciplined minds develop anxious, negative, destructive, irrational thoughts.

I would suggest that calm, positive, constructive, rational thoughts coupled with constructive actions will over time become our new habits and have a greater impact on our lives than anything that actually happens to us. There is no escaping life's challenges; it is, however, during those most difficult times that staying mentally disciplined and controlling our thoughts is the crucial component that will see us through these times. There is no question in my mind that this mental discipline is the major difference between those who lead successful, fulfilling lives, and those who do not.

> It is not the problem; it is how you see the problem. (Einstein)

I think it is also crucial to understand how significant positive self-talk is to our success. Often, throughout the course of the day, our mind is offering us feedback, much of which is counterproductive. One of the major steps in making constructive changes in our lives is to be aware of the self-talk we are having with ourselves and make sure it is productive. It is ironic that we would never allow others to speak to us the way we speak to ourselves. It is crucial that we support ourselves with the self-talk that will assist us in reaching our goals.

Psychologist William James in his book *Positive Addiction* suggested that we are all addicted to something. His premise was that we should choose positive addictions (habits) that will benefit rather than inhibit us in the pursuit of our goals. My assertion is that the most constructive addiction we can cultivate is a strong disciplined mind, which will lead to calm, positive, constructive, rational thoughts, actions, self-talk, and habits.

Change can be difficult, even scary. Strange as it seems, many people would rather stay stuck in uncomfortable counterproductive even dysfunctional situations rather than risk the temporary discomfort of change.

> Growth can be painful, but nothing is more painful than staying stuck where you don't belong. (Mandy Hale)

Hopefully we all realize anything worthwhile requires a certain amount of commitment and work. The concepts presented are simple; the work required will take time and commitment.

> A dream doesn't become a reality through magic, it takes determination and hard work. (Colin Powell)

I would suggest that we eliminate the idea that progress will come immediately. Baby steps will be significant as you secure your footing. This is not a race or a competition with anyone else, rather it is a journey of self-empowerment. Celebrate even small changes, acknowledge your accomplishments, and give yourself credit. It is likely as you progress, your confidence will grow, but along the way, make sure to be your own best friend and encourager with frequent positive self-talk. With practice, it will become a habit.

One of my goals is to make what I present simple in concept, no formulas to memorize, no complex terms, no math. That does not mean that change will be easy, but the fact of the matter is anyone can make the changes necessary to improve their life. The skills presented here have been mastered and incorporated by individuals who possess no greater gifts than you or me. The real key is deciding to make a commitment to yourself and to make real changes in your life.

That's it. The core of what's required to make constructive changes in our lives are:

1. Realize we really only control two things in life, our thoughts and our actions.
2. We must develop a strong disciplined mind in order to control those thoughts and actions.
3. We must make our thoughts calm, positive, constructive, rational.
4. Our self-talk must assist us in reinforcing and securing calm, positive, constructive, and rational thoughts.
5. From our new thoughts and self-talk will flow new feelings and emotions which will replace the old counterproductive thoughts.
6. From here, we will naturally develop new habits that assist us rather than inhibit us.
7. The end result is a changed and improved life.

It is likely you have heard and agreed with much of what has been presented. The dilemma is that understanding is not enough. Regardless of how many books we read, how many seminars we attend, or how pure our intentions, nothing changes until we act.

For change to occur, the principles presented must be practiced and on a regular basis.

> All growth depends on activity, there is no development physically or intellectually without effort and that effort means work. (Calvin Coolidge)

1

Discipline Your Mind
Control Your Thoughts

Simply stated, a disciplined mind is one in which we monitor and control our thoughts. I would suggest that as we begin the process of disciplining our mind and thoughts, we entertain only calm, positive, constructive and rational thoughts. Out of these controlled thoughts will flow constructive actions, useful self-talk, improved feelings and emotions, new and constructive habits, and a changed life. Seems rather simplistic, but those three sentences are the cornerstone of everything I believe and will be presenting in subsequent chapters.

- Discipline your Mind, Control your Thoughts
- Make Your Thoughts Calm, Positive, Constructive, and Rational
- Develop Constructive Actions
- Entertain Useful Self-Talk
- Cultivate New Feelings and Emotions
- Create New Constructive Habits

These concepts work together in a chain reaction helping create a new and enriched life.

I am convinced that the basis of success for those individuals who achieve at the highest levels and who experience happy and fulfilling lives is the ability to discipline their mind.

Let us begin with the premise that there are really only two things we control in life—our own thoughts and our own actions. Many of us spend a significant amount of our lives planning, negotiating, preparing, bargaining, teaching, and attempting to persuade and influence others, and events. I am not suggesting this is a bad thing. On the contrary, there is certainly no harm in trying to influence the outcome of our lives, events, and our world for the better. In fact, these efforts and actions are often quite commendable. Many of mankind's greatest advancements are the result of such actions and efforts. I do, however, think it is crucial to remember that we truly only control our own thoughts and our own actions. Once we accept that fact, we can devote the majority of our time, attention, and energy to what we do have control over, which is how we think and how we act.

It is my contention that if we fail to discipline our mind and control our thoughts and actions, it is unlikely that we will be successful in significantly influencing the things we don't have control over but would like to influence. A person who will not discipline their own mind and control their own thoughts is like a ship without a rudder, drifting aimlessly. As a consequence, the impact they have on any endeavor they undertake will likely be minimal.

A Disciplined Mind
Your Best Friend

The word discipline can be defined in a number of ways. When I ask students to define discipline, they frequently respond with one similar to that found in Webster's Dictionary, "The training of individuals to obey rules or a code of behavior, using punishment to correct disobedience." I think we would agree this is a form of discipline. It is something someone does to us and quite often with unpleasant consequences in an effort to change our behavior. I then direct the conversation to another form of discipline—self-discipline. Obviously, self-discipline is the discipline that is self-imposed, and I would argue is the best kind of discipline because it puts us in charge of the things we actually can control which are our thoughts and our actions. In these two areas, we truly can be the boss. Because so many people are unwilling to take control of their thoughts and actions, their lives feel out of control. In an effort to try and gain some semblance of control and order in their lives, they make the common mistake of trying to change outside events and others. They have failed to grasp the notion that they must first change themselves. These individuals must take control of their thoughts and actions before they can influence events, people, and the world around them. As a general rule, the more control we have in our lives, the more comfortable and secure we feel. As a result, we will have a greater effect in influencing the things that are not in our control.

I cannot emphasize this point enough; if we cannot control our own thoughts and actions, we are unlikely to influence anything else. Once individuals understand this concept, they will likely experience less frustration in their lives. They also come to the realization that they have greater success in influencing events which they would like to change but do not have control over. These individuals can focus their attention on the process of attempting to making constructive changes. Instead of attempting to control the things we have no control over, we would be better served, happier, and more successful in controlling ourselves. I believe self-discipline can and should be a great ally. Discipline, specifically mental discipline, must become a top priority in order for significant change to occur in our lives. As I tell students, discipline is an ally. It is an ally because it helps us get what we want, and when examined in that light goes from being an unwanted burden to becoming a useful tool which helps us achieve our goals. Discipline becomes a friend, and when used consistently is a friend we can count on like no other. Long time Indiana basketball coach Bobby Knight has a definition of discipline which I like:

> Do what you are supposed to do. When you
> are supposed to do it. How you are supposed to
> do it. Every time.

Simple, yes, but also very true. I am convinced; if we follow these four basic tenets of discipline, our chances for success in any endeavor we undertake will be greatly enhanced. If I could para-phrase Bobby Knight's quote, I would suggest the idea of:

> Think what you are supposed to *think*.
> When you are supposed to *think* it. How you are
> supposed to think it. Every time.

Without the mental discipline to control our thoughts, chances of achieving at our highest levels are virtually non-existent. Please keep this one basic thought in mind as we move forward. Having a disciplined mind and controlling our thoughts is absolutely crucial for any of us to make significant life changes and achieve at our highest levels.

> Without the mental discipline to control
> our thoughts, chances of achieving at our highest
> levels are non-existent.

Self-Talk

Psychologists estimate our minds produce some fifty thousand to sixty thousand thoughts daily. Many of these thoughts are random, and a significant number of these thoughts are all too often anxious, negative, destructive, and irrational. The fact is that these negative thoughts influence our attitudes, feelings, emotions, and actions as well as helping color our outlook on life. Coupled with these negative thoughts is our own self-talk in reaction to these ingrained thoughts. Our self-talk frequently confirms the negativity our thoughts present. As a result, we buy into the random destructive thoughts our mind offers, and we develop the mistaken notion we have no control over our thoughts or our life in general. Since we fail to control our own thoughts, we are also likely to develop the ill-conceived notion that we are incapable of handling many of life's challenges. We live in a state of perpetual anxiety, fear, discouragement and even depression. We chastise ourselves for simple everyday mistakes, or inevitable setbacks that subconsciously sabotage our confidence.

Dictionary.com defines self-talk as, "The act or practice of talking to oneself aloud or silently and mentally." With a continual undisciplined mind and accompanying self-talk, it is easy to fall into a downward spiral of destructive thinking and an unfulfilling life. In order to change this cycle of negative thinking and subsequent actions, feelings, and emotions, it is imperative to redirect our thoughts and self-talk. Mental discipline and self-talk work hand in hand. Without a disciplined mind, it is highly unlikely our self-talk—the messages we send to ourselves on a regular basis as well as the picture they paint of ourselves and lives—will become the confidant we can and should be able to rely on. In order to change this destructive cycle, we must begin to monitor and eventually control our thoughts and self-talk. With time and practice, our thoughts and self-talk will become distinctly more calm, positive, constructive, and rational as will our actions, feelings, and emotions.

Fortunately, unless there is some sort of a true mental disorder, we all have the capacity to discipline our mind and control our thoughts and self-talk. The realization that we can control our thoughts and self-talk rather than allowing our thoughts and self-talk to control us is often a paradigm shifting event for many people who are under the mistaken impression that they are the victims of their own thoughts and must stand by passively as their thoughts and self-talk negatively derail their lives. Once we understand and internalize the fact that we can be in control of our thoughts and self-talk, our lives will begin to change for the better. Instead of becoming a victim of our thoughts and the destructive conversations we have with ourselves, we can be aided by these thoughts and conversations. I am convinced that without a strong disciplined mind and constructive self-talk, chances for real change in our lives is highly improbable.

It is my personal opinion that the reason so many people try and fail to make constructive change in their lives, is because they don't recognize that change will only occur if we first change our thoughts and are more aware of what we are telling ourselves with our self-talk. Take a minute to think of all the truly successful people you have observed from various walks of life. It is likely that the vast majority of these individuals have experienced temporary setbacks, disappointment, and failures. In spite of these encounters, they were able to retain a disciplined mind, control their thoughts, use their self-talk to assist them in getting their feeling and emotions in order and move forward with constructive actions and make the adjustments necessary to lead successful lives.

It is difficult to imagine anyone overcoming life's challenges by berating themselves or falling the victim of a negative undisciplined mind and self-talk. Think back on some of the messages you have sent yourself when you made a mistake, had a setback, or prepared for a new challenge. How often have you chastised yourself or questioned whether you could achieve a particular goal. You may have told yourself something like, "I'm not sure I can handle this new project, or I always mess up." Occasionally when I encounter someone with this type of destructive self-talk, I will, just to prove my point, agree with them. "Yes, I think you're right. You clearly don't have what it takes to handle a project of this magnitude. Clearly your boss should have hired someone who is smarter and has more drive and experience than you. This will likely be an unmitigated disaster. You will probably embarrass yourself and the entire organization."

Naturally, I get a quizzical look and frequently a comment, "I thought you were my friend, that wasn't very nice or helpful." Often, after some thought, they get the message. The point I am trying to make is, this is how you sound. This is the nonsense you are telling yourself, and if it came from someone other than yourself, you would rightfully be offended. If it's offensive, hurtful, and counterproductive coming from someone else, then don't say or think it to yourself. Self-Talk must become calm, positive, constructive, and rational.

Monitor Those Thoughts
Think About What You Are Thinking About

It appears to me that one of the primary reasons individuals sabotage their own lives with anxious, negative, destructive, and irrational thoughts and then fail to make the changes they would like to see in their lives is because they have not developed the discipline and created the habit of monitoring their thoughts, actions, and self-talk. The fact is many people simply don't realize how negative and counterproductive their thoughts, actions, and self-talk have become. While there are times we are aware of how destructive our thoughts have become, it is far more common to be completely oblivious to what our mind is messaging us. These thoughts are the result of a lazy, previously undisciplined mind which helped to create these thoughts and habits in the first place. Because of this lack of awareness, we are subject to the frequent mental hijacking which robs us of calm, positive, constructive, and rational thoughts. It is imperative we change this negative cycle with frequent monitoring of our thoughts and actions.

The more we monitor our thoughts and actions and allow only calm, positive, constructive, and rational thoughts to permeate our mind, the stronger we become. Without this monitoring, it is simply too easy to be seduced by the ease of negativity produced by our thoughts, actions and self-talk. As a result, we become more anxious, negative, destructive, and irrational, and our mind becomes weaker and even more undisciplined. Change requires us to discipline our minds and think about what we are thinking about. At first the term, "think what you are thinking about" may seem like an odd phrase, but it really is critical that we are aware of what's taking place in our own mind, and crazy as it sounds, we frequently are not.

To rectify this situation, we must become aware of and consciously reject any and all counterproductive thoughts and replace them with thoughts that will assist us in achieving our goals. As I have stated before, this is really a very simple concept. Simple doesn't mean easy; it requires work. The real work and the key element of making significant life changes requires the mental discipline to monitor what we are thinking about. Some may call it awareness; others call it mindfulness, psychologists call it metacognition, but whatever we call it, we need to know what's going on in our own mind. The upside of monitoring our thoughts and beginning to think about what we are thinking about is so beneficial; so life altering, it is unquestionably worth the effort, and most importantly can be done by anyone.

Human nature, being what it is, encourages us to take the easy way out and allow our thoughts to continue to remain unchecked and lazy thus detouring us from achieving our goals and changing our lives for the better. As a result, our thoughts, actions, and habits remain counterproductive. In the beginning, disciplining our mind and monitoring our thoughts will take time and practice. It is likely that our subconscious mind will try and get us off track with a million and one counterproductive thoughts. The reason for this phenomenon is really quite simple; it is significantly easier to stay where we are, to stay stuck, to choose to be oblivious to what we are thinking. It is always easier to entertain anxious, negative, destructive, and irrational thoughts, than it is to refocus our mind on calm, positive, constructive, and rational thoughts. It takes more discipline and effort to keep our mind strong, than it does to remain weak. To make these changes will require us to pay what seems like an inordinate amount of time and attention to our thoughts.

Early on this process will likely seem tedious. Fortunately, researchers tell us that we can begin to make significant changes in thoughts, actions, and habits within twenty-one days. If worked on diligently, that's how long it takes to begin to make significant changes in our lives. In that short period of time, we can begin to create new thoughts, actions and habits that can literally transform our lives. There are few guarantees in life, but one guarantee is if we fail to monitor our thoughts and self-talk, we will most assuredly stay where we are and fall short of our goals and potential. Remember, in only twenty-one days, we can make significant changes to our thought process and begin to create new and constructive habits. With practice and by following the guidelines outlined in chapter five, change will occur.

Fear No More

Fear frequently precedes failure. Fear begins in our mind. Monitoring our thoughts with a disciplined mind helps reduce fear and doubt. Legendary quarterback Johnny Unitas was asked about throwing what seemed to be a particularly "risky pass" in the closing minutes of the 1958 Championship game. Unitas responded, "It isn't risky if you know what you are doing." That kind of confidence begins in the mind coupled with a constructive self-talk. I think it is highly unlikely in those final minutes Unitas was thinking, "Gosh, I hope I don't throw an interception." In a similar incident, Seattle Seahawks and former USC football coach Pete Carroll recalls the story of coaching Carson Palmer, a highly talented quarterback. Palmer, then the starting USC quarterback, had a terrific spring practice but played poorly in the spring game. In an off-hand remark Palmer commented, "It's just so typical. I always play well but screw up when it matters the most."

Coach Carroll quickly and firmly reminded Carson of one simple fact, "Carson, you never ever get to talk that way again." Coach Carroll in essence had told Palmer, "No negative thoughts, no negative self-talk. Negative talk leads to fear, and fear leads to failure. You need to be more disciplined in your thinking." It is apparent based upon the remainder of his highly successful career as a Heisman Trophy winner and his 15 years in the NFL that Carson Palmer thought more consciously about what he was thinking and saying. It would appear Johnny Unitas had learned that lesson early on. No doubt some individuals come to understand the significance of monitoring what they are thinking early in life. The encouraging fact is that with practice, we can all develop the skill of thought monitoring. There is no question that insecurities and doubt are natural human emotions. The best counter to these mentally created emotions is a reprogrammed thought process coupled with positive self-talk. The good news is every one of us has the ability to do so.

Actions

Most of us expect our actions to assist us in achieving our goals, not deter us.

It is important to understand that these actions begin in the mind. Before a building is built; before the first space shuttle launched, or a business opened, there was a vision with a clear mental picture. This vision led to action. This action was fostered by a disciplined mind, which helped us to stay focused on the objective at hand. This mental vision coupled with constructive action helped create the positive energy necessary to propel that dream to becoming a reality. Disciplining our mind leads to disciplined actions. As we begin to change our actions, they, like our thoughts, will become more calm, positive, constructive, and rational.

Preparation is a crucial form of action. Remember in the Johnny Unitas quote, "If you know what you are doing, it isn't dangerous." Unitas had confidence, not only because of his disciplined mind, but also because of his disciplined actions. Unitas had thrown that pass thousands of times, before, during, and after practice. Legend has it that Unitas and star receiver Ray Berry would spend hours after practice working on just that pattern. The story goes that the two would work by themselves after practice in the dark. They had prepared so diligently that Unitas would throw with such confidence and precision that Ray Berry knew exactly where the pass would be thrown even without seeing it. Unitas knew exactly where Berry would be without actually seeing him. Examples of this type of action (preparation) can be found in all walks of life. World renowned investor Warren Buffet claims he "makes quick decisions, after hours of study." It wasn't just the act of making a huge financial decision that made Warren Buffett one of the richest men in the world. It is the action of preparation that sets Buffett from so many others. The list of successful individuals seem to preach the gospel of study and hard work (action).

Committing to a rigorous work schedule without a disciplined mind is unlikely; a disciplined mind and disciplined action work hand in hand. The disciplined mind assists you in doing the work (action) necessary, and the work (action) helps create the confidence. I would suggest you begin to examine your actions as well as your thoughts. Are your actions assisting you in achieving your goals, and are your thoughts and actions in sync? Study the actions of successful people who you admire and respect. If possible, try and sit down with them even for a few minutes. If that isn't possible, purchase one of their books, attend a seminar, check out YouTube. I can't begin to tell you how many lectures, speeches, news conferences I have studied online of people I admire and enjoy listening to. What these individuals talk about speaks volumes about not only what they think (thoughts) but also what they do (action). The study of these individuals lends credence to the hypothesis that successful, happy, well-adjusted individuals control their thoughts and actions, and generally speaking those thoughts and actions are calm, positive, constructive, and rational. Become a student of successful individuals.

Notice the way they carry themselves. My guess would be they have excellent posture. When they enter a room, they aren't slouched over indicating a lack of confidence. Their entrance probably indicates they are happy to be there, and they feel comfortable interacting with anyone there. I would also assume they have taken the time to clean themselves up and have dressed appropriately. I would bet they have a smile on their face and greet others with a firm handshake or a warm embrace. There is nothing timid in their actions. You might be surprised to know that these individuals likely have or have had, some of the same insecurities as the rest of us, but by acting confidently their mental process changes. Positive thoughts and actions work hand in hand.

Habits

One of the reasons a disciplined mind is a key is that it helps us create new constructive habits that will lead to success. Without being aware, our habits have a powerful and dramatic impact on our lives. They can be destructive, or they can dramatically change our lives for the better. The *American Journal of Psychology* defines habits as "a more or less fixed way of thinking, willing or feeling acquired through previous repetition of a mental experience. New behaviors can become automatic through the process of habit information." In other words, if we keep doing, saying, or thinking something on a consistent basis, it becomes a habit, and something we will likely return to repeatedly without conscious thought, especially in times of stress. Therefore, if practiced consistently, our positive thoughts and actions can become more instinctual.

Constructive change becomes distinctively easier when we create new useful habits. Keep in mind, many of us, over time, have created a weak undisciplined mind and counterproductive actions which have become our habits. My suggestion is we replace the undisciplined mind, negative self-talk, and counterproductive actions with a disciplined mind, constructive self-talk, and productive actions. It is critical that we begin to focus our complete attention to thoughts that will replace the old counterproductive thoughts and actions and create new useful habits. Once I began the process of changing my thoughts, self-talk and actions, I was amazed at how quickly I became aware of what I was thinking, doing, and saying. Very quickly, my habits began to change. If you commit fully to your new focused thought process and actions, you will create habits that assist in reinforcing not only our thoughts, actions, and self-talk but also your feelings and emotions. Changing our thoughts, actions and self-talk is a skill, and like any skill, must be practiced on a consistent basis. When talking with successful individuals, I think you will find they are creatures of habit. Once formed, the habits are almost ritualistic. Whether it is going to the gym for a workout, reading the financial section in the newspaper, prayer or meditation, highly successful people have created habits which aid in their success and happiness. If they are forced to miss part of a daily ritual, they may feel uncomfortable, even a little guilty. Their constructive habits have become part of their life. I'm not talking of neurotic behavior; I'm talking healthy helpful habits. As long as the habits are constructive, this isn't a bad thing. It is a simple reminder they have missed a constructive part of their day. That uncomfortable feeling can be the impetus to keep us moving forward and keeps us on track. Conversely, individuals who have negative habits will likely fall back on their conditioned patterns of behavior which detour rather than assist in their growth and happiness.

Don't Entertain Crooks

In my counseling/coaching sessions, I tell my students that negative thoughts, whether conscious or subconscious, are like thieves.

These negative, counterproductive, irrational thoughts are there to steal your calm, positive, constructive, rational thoughts that will bring happiness, healthy relationships, serenity, success, and most of the good things in life. It would truly be better if a thief were to break into your home and steal your most prized material possessions than to have your calm, positive, constructive, rational thoughts stolen. We can always buy new "things" but losing one's constructive thought process can be difficult to replace.

The more we focus on what we are thinking and allowing only calm, positive, constructive rational thoughts to enter our mind, the stronger it becomes. If we fail to monitor our thoughts, our mind will inevitably gravitate toward anxious, negative, destructive, irrational thoughts and grow weaker and even more undisciplined. In the beginning, disciplining the mind will take time and practice. We will need to pay, what seems to be an inordinate amount and attention to our thoughts, and early on, much like exercise, it may seem like a lot of work, and we may question our progress. Never forget, research tells us that we can begin to make significant changes within only twenty-one days. In that short period of time, we can begin to create new thoughts and habits that can literally transform our lives. The upside of a disciplined mind is huge. Imagine a life of freedom, free of negative, depressive, fearful thoughts, and attitudes that lead to the inevitable self-destructive lifestyle. I remind anyone I counsel/coach, as we go through the transition process, that these changes, while difficult at first, will eventually help us get what we want and in fact disciplining our minds is really the only way to make real lasting change.

Is What I'm Doing Working?

I think it is important as you begin your journey to developing a disciplined mind that you establish specific goals. I would encourage you to decide what makes you happy and fulfilled and not what others view as success. All too often I see individuals who have allowed others to define for them what success is. While many of these individuals may arrive at what others have deemed as successful, they are really not content and fulfilled with their lives. I have seen people who have retired at an early age; others who will never give up work. I have friends who tramp across frozen open fields hunting pheasant, and several buddies who can hit golf balls for hours on end. Some love gardening, some cross-stitch, and some can't wait for the next big sale or merger. The point is what do you want to do, what makes you happy?

I am convinced that the single most important question I ask people with whom I work is, "Is what you are doing working?" If your life is rewarding and fulfilling, if you enjoy what you are doing, and if your relationships are solid, then you are likely on the right track. My guess would be you are probably doing a pretty good job of disciplining your mind. If what you are doing isn't working, if something isn't just right, and something is missing, then it's likely time for a change. Einstein pointed out that the definition of insanity is, "Doing the same thing over and over again and expecting a different result." While it really is common sense, it is important to remind ourselves that if we keep doing the same thing over and over again, we will get the same result. Nothing will change. Again I am thoroughly convinced that the single most important change we can make is our thought process. With a constructive mental shift in thinking, successful outcomes are greatly enhanced. Being a football coach, I remind people that if you run the same play over and over, and you haven't gained a yard, perhaps you need to run another play. Once we have learned to discipline our mind, we are far more likely to act rationally and choose actions which will assist in making choices that will work.

Staying Stuck
There Is No Growth Without Change

It is a remarkable phenomenon that many people would rather stay indefinitely in an uncomfortable, even dysfunctional situation, rather than experience the temporary discomfort of change. Make no mistake, change is hard. While the basic concepts to change are astoundingly simple, the implementation requires great discipline.

This is often the time in a counseling/coaching session where I come to a straightforward decision with students or clients. Are you willing to do what's necessary to make change or not? I frequently qualify that statement by stating that I'm not asking you if you would like to make changes in your life; I'm asking you if you are willing to do what's necessary to make changes. I think it is important to understand wanting something isn't nearly as important as doing something. Remember actions. Nothing changes until you act.

At this point in time, I remind people you have two choices: you can stay where you are, stuck, unhappy, discontented, unfulfilled, or you can deal with the short-term discomfort of change and move forward. I try and be encouraging and remind people they have the power to make these changes. Disciplining our minds, controlling our thoughts, helpful self-talk and changing our habits to becoming more calm, positive, constructive, and rational does not take the intellect of a physicist, or neurosurgeon. It is a definite choice, and it does require work. Fortunately, the discipline to make these changes can be developed with practice. The dirty little secret is that people who decide to change their lives make up their minds to do so and don't relent. Period.

> The dirty little secret is that people who decide to change their lives make up their minds to do so and don't relent. Period.

If a client or student chooses not to work on making changes, okay no hard feelings. We part ways and move on. What I will not do, however, is to allow students/clients to say, "I can't do this." That is simply not true. You can; you are choosing not to. There is a huge difference. We all have the ability to change. It is a choice. I feel it is incumbent upon me to remind students we all have the capacity to make these changes; it is just a matter of fact some people simply choose not to. Once we have established that fact, and the student understands that they are not a victim of uncontrollable circumstances, rather they have consciously made a choice to stay where they are. That way, students/clients are at least empowered with the knowledge that we are responsible for our own condition, not necessarily the circumstances of their life, but they are in control of how they react to and deal with those particular circumstances. If students have that knowledge, even if they choose not to act and make changes at that juncture in their lives, they at least understand that they do have the power. They are also aware of what they need to do at some point in time if they eventually choose to make changes.

All of us, to a greater or lesser degree, have challenges in life. Some challenges are truly tragic, catastrophic events which we have no control over, but we always have control over our reaction to events and circumstances. In Viktor Frankl's book *Man's Search for Meaning,* Frankl describes the horrendous events of a WWII Nazi concentration camp. Despite the unimaginable circumstance, many of these captives pulled together to do whatever they could to assist each other. They made a conscious effort to control their thoughts, and all be it limited, their actions. Whatever path you choose, I hope I have provided you with the knowledge that you do have a choice in taking control of your life.

Principle 1:
Discipline Your Mind
Control Your Thoughts

2

Mentally Strong
Take the Hits

One thing is certain. As we go through life, we will encounter set-backs. No matter who we are—man, woman, rich, poor, regardless of race, religion, or ethnicity—we will all encounter setbacks. Some may be because of our own mistakes, poor choices, or miscalculations. Others may be the result of random circumstances in our life, or because of some injustice perpetrated against us, but without question, successful, happy, well-adjusted individuals have developed the capacity to handle the setbacks, adversity and move on. Like a great boxer, they can take the hits.

> It isn't how hard you can hit. It's how hard
> you can get hit and keep moving forward. That's
> how winning is done. (Rocky Balboa)

It is a fact that successful people have a strong mind that can withstand whatever life throws at them. The higher your goals, the more ambitious your undertaking, the more challenges you will likely encounter. Setbacks in and of themselves are not failure. As long as we continue to adjust our game plan, learn from our mistakes, accept life's injustices, and continue to move forward, we have not failed. It is only when we completely give up on an achievable goal that we have truly failed. The simple truth is that the ability to deal with adversity and keep moving forward separates those who eventually triumph and those who fall short. Many people erroneously assume high achievers and successful people's life journey is a straight line to success, unscathed by problems, disappointment, and heartbreaking experiences. Nothing could be further from the truth. Achieving at the highest levels means we are far more likely to experience more challenges and momentary disappointment than those who choose a less daring road.

I am reminded of San Francisco's Hall of Fame football coach Bill Walsh, who, prior to winning three Super Bowls, experienced repeated setbacks. In fact, three out of four of coach Walsh's first seasons resulted in losing seasons. Coach Walsh recalled a flight returning to San Francisco after yet another disappointing loss. Walsh recalled how he spent virtually the entire flight looking out the window so his players and fellow coaches would not see him crying. While the disappointment was immense, Coach Walsh drew on his mental strength and pressed on. Bill Walsh is just one of thousands of people, who in coaching terms "sucked up the pain" and kept moving forward. The disappointments were no match for coach Walsh's mental strength.

> The successful have failed more times than
> the spectator has tried in their life.
> - Unknown

It is important to be aware of the demanding process, the bumps in the road which high achieving individuals incur. I think we would be better served if we would focus as much time on the challenging process necessary for success as we do sitting back and simply dreaming of the finished product. Clearly, having a specific, clearly-defined goal is crucial for success, but without a realization of the sacrifices and commitment necessary, we only have a wish. Understanding the process and what is necessary is what I refer to as the steps to achieving the goal. As a football coach for over thirty-five years, we would remind our players at the start of each season that everyone wants to stand at midfield after the final game of the year holding the championship trophy overhead and having the first place medal placed around their neck. What was crucial to remember was that before that potentially glorious moment there would be the hours, weeks, months and even years of glamour-less painstaking work, all with no assurance of success. Not only must we never lose sight of our goal. We must also never lose sight of the tireless work, the ability to handle adversity, the disappointments, and setbacks we would likely encounter along the way; they are inseparable. The goal must always be tied to the demanding process. Without mental strength and the ability to take the hits, our ultimate goal is likely unattainable.

In the final analysis, mental strength takes us further than talent alone. There is nothing more common than extraordinarily talented people falling short of their goals because of a lack of mental strength. A strong will with average ability beats superior talent with a weak mind almost every time. A great talent with a strong mind results in superstars in any walk of life. Individuals who ultimately succeed deal with all types of disappointment and adversity, learn from the experience, and move on. Perhaps most importantly high achievers learn to embrace adversity as a propellant for success. Adversity can and should be an exercise in growth. When adversity strikes, rather than complaining, it would greatly benefit us to remind ourselves— here is a valuable learning experience. If dealt with constructively, we will be much farther ahead than if we had never had these experiences. This may sound rather unrealistic, but I can assure you this is exactly what highly successful people do.

The will must be stronger than the skill.
(Muhammad Ali)

I believe adversity can be thought of as mental weight lifting. While lifting weights makes us physically stronger, adversity over time, and if handled properly, makes us mentally stronger. There will most assuredly be discomfort with lifting of weights, and it is not uncommon to question whether our efforts and sacrifices are worth the effort. For those who stick with it, however, within a relatively short period of time, they will literally see their results. The outcomes are observable to the naked eye. The major difference between physical weight lifting and mental weight lifting is that with mental weight lifting, we must make a conscious effort to recognize how our challenges have made us stronger. Without that recognition, we miss an excellent learning opportunity and chance for growth.

It is not uncommon, after a difficult experience, to think, "I'm glad that's over." I would recommend, instead, we look back at any difficult or unpleasant experience and compliment yourself on a job well done. Remind yourself, however painful the situation was, in spite of all that you encountered, you were able to weather the storm and fight on and achieve your goal. Even if you fell short of your goal, give yourself credit for hanging in there and finishing the task at hand. The outcome of any event is not nearly as important as the commitment you made to it, and the persistence and resilience demonstrated. We will not win every battle, but if we keep battling, in the long run, we will come out with more wins than losses, and our lives will be significantly more fulfilling.

Take a minute and think of someone you have learned from. They may have been a classroom teacher, coach, boss, parent, or friend. Most likely, they pointed out ways you might improve in some endeavor, or pointed out an error, that if corrected would lead to your becoming more productive, efficient, and successful. They may have been kind, patient, and subtle in their direction, or they may have been stern and abrupt. The manner the message was delivered was irrelevant. The point is there were tangible lessons learned which assisted you in moving forward. Like a good teacher, adversity can help us learn. We can make adjustments and move on better equipped to handle life's next challenge or opportunity. With each obstacle we hurdle, the mentally stronger and more confident we become. If we succumb to adversity, we grow weaker and less sure of ourselves and our abilities. The act of moving forward regardless of the outcome builds strength.

Nothing in the world can take the place of persistence (Mental Strength). Talent will not; nothing is more common than unsuccessful men with talent. Genius is not; unrewarded genius is almost a proverb. Education will not; the world is full of educated derelicts. Persistence and determination alone are omnipresent. The slogan "press on" has always solved the problems of the human race. (Calvin Coolidge)

One of my favorite antidotes about dealing with adversity comes from Thomas Edison who had an innovative way of looking at life's challenges. When working on the incandescent light bulb, it reportedly took Edison ten thousand tries before he perfected his technique. When asked by a reporter how it felt to have failed 9,999 times, Edison replied, "I never failed. I simply discovered 9,999 ways that didn't work." I believe part of the process of dealing with adversity is to accept setbacks as a necessary and inevitable step along our path to success. It would be in our best interest to endure setbacks, as did Edison, and allow these stumbling blocks to assist us on our journey to greater success. Let's be realistic, many of life's hard-learned lessons, at the time, are unwelcome events. However, these events, when viewed as a learning experience, can eventually take us to a higher level of achievement and can be dealt with in a more constructive manner. I cannot overstate this point too much; this is how the minds of successful, high achieving, well-adjusted people work.

Basketball great Michael Jordan had a similar perspective. "I missed 900 shots in my career, lost almost 300 games, 26 times I was trusted to make the winning shot and missed. I failed over and over again in my life. That's why I succeeded." While I wouldn't choose the word failed to describe his temporary setbacks, I believe the principle remains the same. What doesn't kill us makes us stronger if we continue to press on regardless of the circumstances. Jordan had another quote that epitomizes his incredible mental strength. "When I miss a shot at a crucial time, my mind immediately flashes back to a time when I made a crucial shot. Most people can't do that." What an insightful statement, "most people can't." In my opinion the reason they "can't" is because they have not developed the mental strength necessary to do so. They have not embraced the concept that adversity will assist them in developing the mental toughness to endure the most challenging of times. The good news is we all possess the ability to develop that mental strength. It would serve us well to emulate the Michael Jordans of the world and accept adversity as an opportunity to develop greater mental strength.

There are numerous synonyms for mental strength. Grit is a word defined by Angela Duckworth as "one of the greatest indicators of success." I had never given much thought to the word "grit" other than it was in the title of the classic John Wayne movie *True Grit.* To my surprise, psychologists have long referred to grit as: Perseverance and passion for long term goals. Individuals who exhibit characteristics and traits of grit outperform peers of equal intelligence and may be the greatest indicator of success. That to me is an extraordinary statement and seems to support much of what I believe. Fight through the hard times, don't quit, and you will likely finish ahead of those who may have greater gifts but lack the mental strength and resolve to fight through the difficult times.

Grit...may be the greatest indicator of success. (Angela Duckworth)

The Finnish have what has become one of my favorite words—*sisu.* Translated *sisu* means: "the ability to act in the face of adversity, repeated failure, and overwhelming odds." The word *sisu* dates back five hundred to six hundred years but drew world notoriety in 1939 when the Soviet Union with its 2.5 million man army invaded Finland with only 810,000 men to defend itself. Despite the massive manpower and advance air superiority of the Soviet Union, the tiny country of Finland held their ground and earned a peace accord while relinquishing only a small portion of land. I have always been a firm believer in positive thinking and view it as a crucial element for success. *Sisu* however takes the thinking process a step farther and requires us to act. As you may recall, I stated in chapter one that it is my belief that we control only two things in life, our thoughts and our actions. *Sisu* calls us to act. This action is the behavioral aspect of what we control and assists us in further developing mental strength. Over time, all of us have the capacity to develop the fortitude and courage to confront fear, pain, danger, uncertainty, intimidation, shame, and discouragement. Mentally strong people refuse to blame others or make excuses. They refrain from being overly critical of themselves, others, or circumstances. They most definitely refuse to allow themselves to become victims. These individuals continue to put one foot in front of the other, put their head down and go. While individuals with this great mental strength are not the norm, this skill can be learned and developed. It does require focus and repeated practice.

We all know change can be difficult, and it would benefit us to frequently remind ourselves that we all possess the capacity for that change. Once we reprogram our thoughts and remind ourselves that every obstacle we encounter helps makes us stronger, the easier change becomes. Disciplining our mind will help keep us focused and on track. There is a coaching axiom that states we learn more from losing than from winning, and unfortunately, this is probably true. While losing is painful, when used constructively, it allows us to point out weakness, flaws, and if corrected, will make us even better than before.

In our high school guidance center, we had a poster of Franklin Roosevelt, Harry Truman, Theodore Roosevelt, and Dwight D. Eisenhower. Rather than a list of the accomplishments each of these historical figures had achieved, there was a list of setbacks each had encountered throughout their lives. I might add, the list for each was quite lengthy. It was a perfect illustration to our students, and a reminder to all of us, that the road to success is filled with stumbling blocks, even for presidents. The temptation to throw in the towel was no less pressing for these great leaders than for you or me. Instead, they endured the pain, disappointment and continued on, and because of their perseverance, they prevailed. And I might add, because of their efforts, we are all the beneficiaries of their mental strength. Winston Churchill had enumerable famous quotes but my favorite has always been, "Never give in never, never, never, never, in nothing great or small, large or petty never give in...never yield to the apparent overwhelming might of the enemy." I would suggest we follow Churchill's advice and never run from pressure-filled situations of adversity. It is human nature to try and remove ourselves from stressful, emotionally painful, or unpleasant situations. It is, however, at these times we learn the most and develop maximum mental strength.

13 Things Mentally Strong People Don't Do
Amy Morin

1. They don't waste time feeling sorry for themselves.
2. They don't give away their power (because they know they can control their emotions).
3. They don't shy away from change, they realize change is inevitable. And they believe in their ability to adapt.
4. They don't waste energy on things they can't control.
5. They don't worry about pleasing everyone.
6. They don't fear taking calculated risks.
7. They don't dwell in the past.
8. They don't make the same mistake over and over.
9. They don't resent other people's success.
10. They don't give up after the first setback.
11. They don't fear time alone.
12. They don't feel the world owes them anything.
13. They don't expect immediate results.

Principle 2:
Stay Mentally Strong
Take the Hits

3

Positive Constructive Rational

In chapter one, I suggested, as we begin the process of disciplining our mind, we choose to keep our thoughts calm, positive, constructive, and rational. In this chapter, I would like to focus on positive, constructive, and rational thoughts. Chapter four will be devoted completely to calm thoughts and mind. While I am sure most of us have a reasonable understanding of the words, positive, constructive, and rational, I think it would be helpful for me to elaborate and clarify these terms as I view them so we will all understand not only what each word means but also what each word does not mean.

The word positive is often associated with confidence, optimism, and the ability to affirm and find something good in any given situation. Constructive is defined as helpful, productive, useful, and aiding in improvement. Rational is logical, realistic, sensible, and sound. There is no question, whatever circumstances we find ourselves, our life will dramatically change for the better if we keep our thoughts and actions positive, constructive, and rational.

While being positive encourages us to look at the upside of any situation we encounter, it is most definitely not a Pollyanna philosophy. Being positive doesn't mean we assume we will breeze through life without challenges or problems. Nor does being positive mean our problems will suddenly vanish. As I tell my clients, positive thinking isn't rainbows, fluffy clouds, and unicorns. Part of being positive is the ability to remain constructive and rational in our thinking, realizing we will all have problems, challenges, and setbacks. The true positive thinker recognizes this and has the inner strength to believe above all else, "I can deal with any situation, circumstance, or event which life throws at me."

> Staying positive doesn't mean you will always be
> happy. It means that even on your hardest days
> you know there will be better ones to come.
> - Lovonda Murphy

In the last chapter, we discussed being mentally strong and having the ability to take the hits. What a positive, constructive, rational thought process does is help us deal with and work through unpleasant circumstances. It is not pretending problems do not exist or will never arise. Without question, we have all experienced events in our lives where we were convinced that there was no path forward; only to discover circumstances changed, and events were not as dire as we had imagined. It is possible things were not as we had hoped or envisioned, but there was still a satisfactory, or at least, some path forward. Positive thinking is not pretending there are no problems, but instead having enough mental strength and discipline to help provide us with the hope and faith in ourselves to find whatever sliver of silver lining there might be in the darkest of clouds. We are also likely to discover, when life becomes particularly hard, our positive attitude will assist us in persevering and identifying constructive and rational alternatives thus assisting us in remaining mentally strong.

Consider the individual who loses a job which they enjoyed and seemed to be perfectly suited for, only to find that a new more lucrative opportunity presented itself. Positive, constructive, rational individuals are able to avoid catastrophic thinking and retain their rational thought process rather than relying on emotion. I can assure you when I become overly emotional and begin to entertain worst case scenario, I have almost always diverted my thinking away from rational thoughts. Remaining rational assists us in exploring options. It is helpful in moving forward. Therefore, it is also constructive.

Positive, constructive, rational individuals know as they move through life that they will likely have to adjust what they are doing, and they are aware they will likely have to come up with contingency plans. Realizing that basic concept is tremendously constructive. It helps us deal with the inevitable challenges we will face along the way. Walt Disney said, "I always look on the optimistic side, but I'm realistic (rational) enough to know life is complex." Not only is that thinking positively and rationally, it is constructive; because it reminds us as we go through life, we will likely need to alter our plans and develop the ability and the skill of adjusting on the run. Winning coaches and successful business men and women know that those who have the ability to adjust their game plan the quickest will inevitably be the most successful. As coaches, we wanted our players to be positive and confident. What we didn't want were daydreamers.

People who live in a fantasy world are not positive, constructive or rational thinkers. Thinking we will achieve our goals without challenges is in no way constructive; because at the first setback or difficulty, they become discouraged and frequently quit. Positive, constructive and rational individuals prepare for the inevitable, a challenge, a setback or a bump in the road. It is completely constructive and rational to prepare ourselves mentally for any and all challenges we are likely to face. We wanted our athletes to be thoroughly prepared for any challenge they encounter, and that most definitely included mental challenges. That's positive, constructive, and rational.

As we began a new season or prepared for a game, we never wanted our athletes to picture a walk in the park. We wanted our players to know our opponent's strengths and their weaknesses, as well as respecting everyone we played, regardless of their record. We assumed and coached our athletes to expect our opponent's best effort. Throughout the week of preparation, our coaches would incorporate a drill period called sudden change. As our offensive team ran through their plays, a coach would yell fumble or interception. Immediately our defensive unit would run onto the field so we could practice an unexpected, unwanted turnover. That's not negative; that's preparation, mental preparation.

The objective was that during a game if we did turn the ball over to our opponent, rather than reacting negatively, we would be prepared to act constructively to this unwanted hurdle. Since we had practiced this sudden change, we were prepared mentally to deal with it. It is the same concept as having a fire drill. The goal is to remain calm in a difficult situation, which is in and of itself positive, constructive, and rational. It is helpful and logical. We were confident, that because throughout the week, we had practiced every possible scenario that might arise during the game; we would react well. We prided ourselves on never losing our composure throughout the game, especially when adversity struck. The principal is the same. In any endeavor or undertaking we need to be positive, constructive and rational, and we do this by preparing for inevitable challenges, and we need to prepare on a regular basis.

Over the years, I have developed a list of characteristics that positive, constructive, and rational people exhibit. In general, these people see possibilities whereas individuals with a negative, destructive, irrational mindset only see problems. Positive, constructive, rational individuals are also quicker to forgive themselves and others for mistakes or insults. Holding grudges, resentment, or reliving past mistakes is negative, destructive, and irrational. It serves no purpose. Positive, constructive, and rational individuals are optimist as well as realistic. They have developed the capacity to remain logical in the face of adversity. They are more resilient and less likely to quit. Perhaps as a result of their more productive outlook, they are sound sleepers, less stressed, more grateful, and altruistic, have more energy, and exercise more. When you look at it from a completely rational standpoint, why wouldn't we choose that mental thought process and lifestyle. Notice I said choose because it is a choice. Without being overly critical of our negative, destructive, irrational friends, they do seem to have a problem for every solution. They tend to be overly critical of themselves and others thus limiting their vision and focus.

Negative, destructive, irrational thinkers tend to see dead ends where their more successful friends see a momentary detour which may take them on a new exciting, and perhaps more productive journey. Our negative, destructive, irrational thinking friends would do well to listen to the words of Theodore Roosevelt who encouraged us to "go after our dreams with passion and purpose even if you don't know how you will achieve them, the answer will show up along the way." That strikes me as being positive, constructive, and rational and a wonderful way to lead our lives.

There is a natural tendency for people to wait until things are perfect before they act or undertake a new endeavor. The fact is that in most new undertakings, things are almost never perfect. The time is never exactly right.

I'm not sure why it is but negative, destructive, irrational thinkers have a greater fear of accepting new challenges. They seem to have an inordinate fear of setbacks. My theory is that this is partly because these people care too much what others think, and the thought of anyone criticizing them seems unbearable. It is also possible these individuals are perfectionists, and as a result realize they cannot live up to their own unrealistic expectations. It is also possible they fail to draw on past successes. In spite of the fact these individuals have likely had numerous successes, they may feel they were just lucky. While their success was hard earned, they fail to give themselves credit for prior accomplishments. Most likely, they have simply conditioned their thoughts and focus on what could go wrong and be lost, rather than what could go right and be gained.

Whatever the cause, negative, destructive, irrational thinkers waste valuable time and energy fighting phantom catastrophes or avoiding potential problems, that may never present themselves or even exist. Positive, constructive, rational thinkers are less likely to delay beginning new projects or taking on new challenges. They understand a contest was never won by sitting on the sideline. They realize that there simply isn't a perfect time or place for any new idea or project but dive in anyway. They try, and perhaps have momentary setbacks, but without question, they learn what works and what doesn't work and move on. Not only are they none the worse for the wear, but they are more prepared and more knowledgeable because of these learning experiences. And obviously, they are miles ahead of those who have yet to begin their journey.

I worked for a principal who, whenever we started a new project would say, "We will try this, and if it doesn't work, we'll back up and go down another road." He was a great person to work for because he believed in excellence and wasn't afraid of having to readjust our course of action. There was no question we would reach our goals one way or another because we would keep trying and keep learning every step along the way. Along these lines, I think it is important as we begin the process of making changes in our life that we set realistic goals. It is wonderful to set our sights on being the next Warren Buffett, but it might be wise to begin by first balancing the family checkbook. I believe this would come under the heading of rational.

I would never discourage anyone from setting incredibly lofty goals. When students come to me and say they plan to play in the NFL, attend an Ivy League school, or be a captain of industry, I never discourage them. I do however suggest a step-by-step plan (which we will discuss in chapter five) beginning on the ground floor. I would lay out what I had seen successful athletes, students, and businessmen and women do. I think some people become discouraged because they fail to take into account that their journey will likely begin with a mundane day-to-day process. Starting at the lowest levels, learning the basics and persevering is not a bad thing; it is all part of the process. I feel it is an important part of my job to outline what these individuals will need to commit to in order to achieve their goals.

I'm very proud of my two sons who are very successful and respected in their respective businesses. My oldest is a realtor in Phoenix. Prior to entering the real estate business, he worked new home construction. During the early 2000's, business was very profitable. When the recession hit, construction jobs dried up. At the worst time possible with the housing market at its lowest point nationally and especially in the Phoenix area, he earned his real estate license and began selling homes. The early years were a struggle. He began selling forty-thousand-and fifty-thousand-dollar homes and was happy to have the few sales he did. He worked hard to develop his own specific plan, and gradually as the market recovered, his business took off. He was able to set realistic goals, deal with the challenges of poor economic conditions, take the hits, stay strong, and create a very successful business. My youngest son is today a successful general manager of a prestigious country club in Omaha. His career path began as outside service personnel at a local municipal golf course. His responsibilities included cleaning golf carts, emptying waste baskets and vacuuming the pro shop, and yes, cleaning restrooms. Over time, he became the assistant professional. From there, he moved on to the assistant professional job at the country club, then head professional, and eventually the general manager. The point is both boys began from the ground up. And believe me when I say there was nothing at all glamorous about their beginning, but they worked hard wherever they were. They stayed positive, constructive, and rational, and gradually, the quality of their careers improved.

Every championship team I have coached or studied began by practicing basic fundamentals. The goal of a championship was always there, but everyone involved coaches and players alike knew the journey began and ended with plain old-fashioned boring fundamentals and hard work. Those fundamentals were practiced over and over again under the hot August sun and ending in the frigid cold of November.

Truly Catastrophic Events

The things I have discussed up until now are basically normal life experiences. Unfortunately, there are times in our lives where we encounter truly catastrophic events. The loss of a loved one, a debilitating injury, a disease, or a life threatening illness. Things that shake us to the core. Truly life altering events. For some, the question becomes, does positive, constructive, rational thinking work for life's most challenging situations? My contention is that it is at these most difficult times we must be at our strongest and remain positive, constructive, and rational.

I think of a colleague, a wonderful high school counselor, Kristen Glasser, one of the finest educators I had the pleasure to work with. Her husband was a beloved police officer in Phoenix who was fatally shot, leaving her with two small children. Since that time, Kristen has worked tirelessly and began the Dave Glasser Foundation to assist at-risk students with athletic and mentoring programs run by Phoenix Police officers. In discussing her commitment to this endeavor, Kristen commented, "Something positive must come out of this." At times like this, we can surrender our lives to despair and depression or find something to draw upon to keep us going. No one I have encountered exemplifies this better than Kristen Glasser.

I often struggled with what to say or what advice to offer to individuals who have lost a loved one or are experiencing a true traumatic event. Words at this time seem so insufficient, and the advice, which I believe is fundamentally sound, seems hollow. What I have discovered and one of the reasons I believe so strongly in what I'm presenting here is, that staying positive, constructive, and rational, really is our best, and perhaps our only option. When I see people suffering and experiencing unbelievable hardship, I frequently ask myself what possible positive can come from a tragic situation. I have come to the conclusion that the first positive a person can draw upon is, "I can get thru this. Somehow, someway I will put one foot in front of the other and live one day, one hour, one minute at a time and get through this." That single simplistic positive thought process in and of itself becomes constructive and rational. While in the midst of a truly unimaginable tragic event, this thought process may assist us because it may be all we have.

I remember a young student whose father had passed away. Naturally, she was distraught. We visited a few times where we talked about the grieving process and how she might best deal with this traumatic event. Each time she left, it seemed to me, feeling no better, and while I knew time would be her best friend, I still felt very inept as a counselor and what I was offering. A month later, she came back into visit and commented, "Something you said helped." I wondered what I possibly could have said that helped because nothing that I could recall seemed very inspirational to me. When I asked what I had offered, she commented that I had advised: "Sometimes when you are going thru hell, you just keep going." This still doesn't strike me as being terribly inspirational, but I do think it supports the idea that sometimes in the most dire of circumstances, keeping positive, constructive, and rational means we just keep going and doing the best we can.

I hope these thoughts reinforce my hypothesis that positive, constructive, rational thinking isn't just living in a state of denial or unrealistic optimism. True positive, constructive, rational thinking is simple in concept, but it takes hard work and practice. Fortunately, we all possess that ability.

Principal 3:
Foster Positive Constructive Rational Thoughts

4

A Calm Mind

> When you can't control what's happen-
> ing, challenge yourself to control the way you
> respond. That's where the power is. (Unknown)

One trait I have always admired in successful, happy, well-adjusted individuals is their ability to maintain a true sense of inner calm in the face of adversity. I am fascinated when observing truly successful people in the moment of perceived or actual calamity or crisis. It is rare to witness a truly successful person act in a frantic, anxious or irrational manner. Successful individuals are not easily upset or overly agitated by problems, or an unfortunate turn of events. I have observed successful individuals who while momentarily upset, regain their sense of calm despite the pressure of a situation. Obviously, we all become upset, but highly efficient people have developed the ability to deal with the annoyances, challenges, and crises which life throws at them and quickly return to a sense of calm and composure.

One highly successful businessman I know explained to me that when stressful situations arise, "Rather than panicking, exploding, and losing control of my thoughts and actions, I intentionally quiet my mind, speak in quieter tones and with less emotion. To help deal with the stress of any given situation I intentionally slow my actions, take a few deep slow breaths, and relax my hands, arms, and shoulders. I make every effort to respond by becoming rational and acting with a calm mind rather than unchecked emotions. I try and listen and gather as much information as possible. I make it a point to never act while agitated or anxious."

The greatest golfer of all time, Jack Nicklaus commented, "I learned early on I couldn't play well when I was excited, so I learned to make myself calm." Clearly those who handle stressful situations best operate from a calm, rational mind. Like Jack Nicklaus, we too can learn to make ourselves calm in stressful situations. Individuals who have developed the skill of remaining calm, explore options, and make decisions based on facts and data, not emotions. Calm thoughts are our best defense against irrational emotions. Calm individuals can express their ideas, disagreement, or displeasure without escalating the situation. This calm demeanor often helps those around them remain calm in a difficult situation and provides an atmosphere and environment for constructive action. It is during the direst of times, we need to seek information, data, and facts to make the best out of any situation.

I think you are likely to discover that we will solve more problems and win more discussions with an open mind and soft hand rather than a clenched fist and a loud voice. In any challenging or crisis situation, remaining calm invariably prevails over a loss of composure. That seems obvious, but we are all human and our emotions, at times, can get the best of us. It is important to note that remaining calm in challenging times or a crucial situation is a skill. It first begins in the mind, and with continual practice can become a constructive habit. It is only common sense that we are more likely to experience greater success if we are able to think clearly, make decisions, and express our emotions calmly and succinctly. Every chaotic experience we face is a chance to practice developing our sense of inner calm.

I have mentioned this before, but I think it bears repeating, every challenging situation we face is an opportunity to practice getting better. The key is to recognize these moments as opportunities. Time spent being upset, angry, or in panic mode is time diverted from growing and problem solving. There is an old coaching axiom: "If you are yelling, you are not coaching." As a rule, being excessively upset is time misspent. In the next chapter, I will lay out a plan for monitoring your progress, but for now keep in mind that those individuals who have developed inner and outer strength usually do not find themselves overreacting, and return as quickly as possible to calm, positive, constructive, rational thinking and the task at hand.

Equanimity

Equanimity is defined as: "Mental calmness, composure and evenness of temper, especially in a difficult situation." Equanimity is what I personally strive for. Notice I said strive for. Like many of the things discussed in this book, they are a work in progress. When used properly, however, equanimity assists me in retaining a calm, positive, constructive, rational mind which in turn helps me in making logical and productive decisions.

Individuals who exhibit equanimity seem to develop an enhanced sense of self awareness. They are aware of triggers which might cause them to lose their sense of calm and composure. I continue to be impressed with those who, although agitated or upset remain calm and act rationally despite the circumstances or situations. Losing one's composure is like pouring gas on a fire—counterproductive.

Frequently individuals who lose their sense of calm and equanimity fall into catastrophizing. In this state, the undisciplined mind loses the sense of calm and begins to panic. Catastrophizing is the complete loss of mental discipline which results in our being overrun by wild worst case scenarios. When caught up in this mental disharmony, not only do our thoughts begin to race but our body begins to overreact as well. Our pulse and heart rate quicken as our breathing becomes rapid and shallow, and our blood pressure rises. We may feel light headed, even nauseous. Adrenaline can transform our bodies into a fight or flight mode. Rational thoughts begin to shut down as negative emotions flood our body. If you have ever been in a fender bender, you may have experienced some of these feelings and emotions. Rather than immediately picturing the worst case scenarios, this is when it would be more useful to think logically. No one appears to be seriously injured, and while there may be unpleasant consequences, such as higher insurance premiums, our car being in the repair shop, cost of a rental car, this will likely pass within a week or month, and life will return to normal and overtime be forgotten. Granted this is not a typical reaction, but it would be a far more useful reaction than panicking.

A fender bender is a relatively mundane situation compared to some of life's truly colossal events. Imagine Pearl Harbor or 9/11. Regardless of politics, George Bush's remarks while standing on the rubble of the World Trade Center after 9/11 were given high marks by many Americans at helping restore a sense of calm, as was Franklin Roosevelt's talk to the nation after Pearl Harbor. In fact, it is at times like this that drawing on our mental strength and remaining calm will be one of our greatest allies. In real crisis situations, we must focus on what we can do now, at this very moment. Our minds must be consumed with the task at hand and not make the situation even worse by panicking and letting our thoughts run wild.

In a true crisis situation, we must stay completely in the present. After the fact, we will have time to evaluate and access the effects of events, but in the moment, we must act in the most efficient, calmest manner possible. Whenever a worst case scenario presents itself, we must ask ourselves the rhetorical question, "How will losing my composure help this situation?" Obviously, this is easier said than done. It must be practiced. This is why any smaller annoying situation is an excellent opportunity to begin the practice of staying calm. Whenever things appear to be at their worst is when we must be at our calmest and most disciplined mentally. We have to draw on any positives we can muster. It is at just these times we must control our thoughts and mind, or our thoughts will control us.

Worry

One of the best pieces of advice I have come across to assist me in remaining calm comes from Dale Carnegie's book, *How to Stop Worrying and Start Living*. Carnegie suggested in a crisis situation we examine the circumstances and evaluate what's the worst that can happen and accept it. "Once we have accepted the worst case scenario, we are then freed to allow ourselves to begin to think and act rationally and move forward because we have mentally accepted what has happened." We are free to begin to think logically and decide what we can do from this point in time forward. I like to remind myself that worry won't prevent bad things from happening or solve a problem. I am convinced that some people use worry as a defense mechanism to ward off negative events.

This type of thinking becomes a superstitious ritual which is a guaranteed way to destroy our calm mind. If and when you begin to panic, try and remind yourself that calm, rational thinking, and actions are really our most effective resources in difficult times.

A real life example of remaining calm in a true crisis situation was experienced by Jack Stark. Jack has been a highly regarded clinical psychologist with a private practice and has gained much notoriety as a sports psychologist working with college and professional sports teams as well as NASCAR. In his book, *The Championship Formula,* Dr. Stark divulged how the day before he was to take his doctoral exams, Jack's infant son was diagnosed with a disease which would greatly restrict a normal life and shorten his life expectancy. It would require far more time and energy on the part of Jack and his wife. You can only imagine the shock and disbelief upon receiving such horrendous news. To make matters worse, there was no way to reschedule his exams; he would need to begin testing the next day. As I read Jack's recollections of that day, I found myself thinking, I don't think I would have been able to go on. I'm afraid that situation would have crippled me. Dr. Stark, however, drew on every bit of the mental strength he could summon, and with a calm mind took his exams and earned his doctorate.

Jack had to put aside panic, worry, and fear to focus on what he could control, and a calm mind was a crucial element in that process. By remaining calm, Dr. Stark was able to deal with a gut-wrenching experience and as a result was able to devote much of his adult life to helping others. In a calm productive manner, he accepted what he could not control and focused on what he could control. When I think of Jack Stark's situation and the hundreds and thousands of others who experience real life crisis situations, I am reminded of a quote by President Teddy Roosevelt: "Do what you can where you are with what you have."

Worry less and do more is always good advice. I try and remember that whenever I become agitated, or I'm presented with a difficult situation. Over the years, I have learned losing my composure and sense of calm is never productive and invariably makes matters worse. This statement, like much of what I'm offering, is so basic, and obvious it seems to go without saying. The fact is, however, that we often fail to heed the most fundamental information which can help us the most. Knowing however isn't enough. We need to put it into practice.

Remaining calm and composed can truly be our greatest asset in a challenging or crisis situation. In fact, there may be times, where a calm mind is our only asset. To help me in any difficult situation, I try and remind myself, whatever I encounter, whatever the magnitude of the situation, I only control two things, my thoughts and my actions. Attempting to control things beyond our control only leads to frustration and the loss of calm and well-being. In order to maintain that sense of calm, our thoughts must remain rational, and our actions should be slowed.

Excellence Not Perfection

As I have previously mentioned, setting a goal of perfection is a surefire way to destroy your sense of calm. To me, the goal of striving for excellence is always a more productive avenue. The burden of being perfect is literally too much for anyone to carry over an extended period of time. Not only is it exhausting, in my opinion, it can lead to discouragement and even depression. Life can be challenging enough; don't make it any harder with impossible expectations.

Anxiety

Anxiety is a real problem for many people. There are valid reasons to be anxious. New challenging situations, dangerous endeavors can create anxiety. I had a friend who went from being a highly successful high school football coach to serving as assistant coach at a perennial powerhouse Division I football program. When I asked him how he was enjoying the new challenge, he stated, "It's great. I just wish I could relax." Seems to me, a change of that magnitude would be an understandable cause for momentary anxiety. I have friends who have skydived and bungee jumped. In these situations, we know the cause of our anxiety.

There are other times where we experience anxiety, but we really are not sure why. There appears to be no real reason for our anxiousness. Psychologists refer to this as free-floating anxiety. While we experience a general sense of nervousness, there is no real impending danger. When these situations arise, I suggest to my students to ask themselves, "Why am I anxious, why am I nervous?" That question helps us return to rational thinking, and can also help us return to a calmer thought process. While realizing there is no real reason for our anxiety may not in and of itself stop our nervousness, it does help us to think what we are thinking about. This refocused thinking can assist us in redirecting our thoughts in a more constructive direction and gradually lead to a reduction in anxiety.

I believe strongly that caring excessively about what other people think of us is another cause of anxiety. I often ask clients, "Why do you care so much about what others think of you?" When you care excessively what others think of you, they have the power and control over you. You actually relinquish your power and control to other people. Remember one of our primary goals is to control what we can. How we feel about ourselves is definitely within our control. As a general rule, trying to control things that are not within our control causes anxiety. I would again recommend you evaluate what you can control and accept the rest.

A Higher Power
Acceptance

While I am definitely no expert in religion, I have observed that people with a disposition for faith frequently seem to have a sense of calm about them. My theory is that because we control so little in our lives, it is comforting to believe there is some sort of logic and order to our world. Trusting in a divine being helps us to accept what we cannot control. Acceptance of what we cannot change is instrumental in creating that sense of calm. Acceptance in psychological terms is a person's assent to the reality of any situation, recognizing a process or condition without attempting to change or protest it.

"Let go and let God" is a noted Christian phrase which reminds us to turn over what we cannot control to a higher power. "God, grant me the serenity to accept the things I cannot change: the courage to change the things I can: and the wisdom to know the difference," was a prayer my father would often recite. It appears to me this is not only a calming prayer but also is a constructive thought process. One thing my dad would remind me as I was growing up was, "Fight it as hard as you can then let it go." I have no intention of standing by passively if there is any indication I can alter the outcome of a situation for the better. However, if I have taken every possible course of action, and the outcome is irrevocable, then I must accept it. I let it go. To do otherwise would be an exercise in futility. Another biblical expression along the same line is "having done all stand." All of these quotes say to me that we are to do everything we can to enhance our lives, and the lives of others for the better, but in the final analysis, the only things we control are our thoughts and actions; the rest we must accept. When we have done all we can and accept the outcome whatever it may be, we will likely find ourselves in a state of calm. From here, we are free to move on to make the best of what we can.

> Acceptance of what has happened is the first step to overcoming the consequences of any misfortune. (William James)

While being Christian myself, I have discovered that reading Buddhist Philosophy helps provide me with a sense of calm. In fact, a great deal of Buddhist teaching is dedicated to maintaining a calm mind, which Buddhists have discovered helps make life not only more enjoyable but also more productive and helpful to themselves and others. One interesting aspect of Buddhist Philosophy is that the harder we fight worry, panic, fear, or nervousness, the worse our situation appears. As a result, our actions become less productive, and our lives more anxious. Buddhists would recommend that rather than fighting these emotions, we acknowledge them, accept them, and allow them to roll off our back or simply melt away. Buddhists are able to accomplish this partly by relaxing the mind and the body. The calmer the mind, the more likely an unpleasant situation may be improved or possibly averted, and or dealt with in a constructive, rational manner.

I am sure I am not the only person to have created crises in my mind which never occur. I wonder how much time and energy I have spent fighting imaginary battles and how much better this time might have been spent. Life can be challenging enough without creating problems in our mind that don't exist, or may never present themselves. It makes no sense practicing being worried, angry, anxious, or upset. If and when we encounter a difficult situation, it makes far more sense to remain calm and allow our rational mind to take over. It doesn't take a rocket scientist to recognize a calm demeanor will carry us farther than anxious, negative, destructive, irrational thoughts. I would like to reiterate that having a calm mind does not mean being weak or lacking a competitive spirit. Quite the opposite.

Calming our mind actually puts us in the optimal mental state to pursue and achieve our lofty goals. Eleven-Time NBA Champion Coach Phil Jackson is often referred to as the Zen Master because of his Buddhist Meditation practices. Coach Jackson also incorporates Native American spiritual practices to assist him in keeping his mind calm and focused. I don't think anyone would view Phil Jackson as lacking competitive spirit. Rather he understands a calm mind works better in a pressure situation than does a frantic, panic-stricken mind. Always keep in mind, acceptance is a key element in developing calm mind. If a particular battle is lost, learn and move on. Don't try and fix the unfixable.

One key word I have used several times in this chapter is practice. For me, remaining calm in a crisis situation is anything but natural. I need to practice remaining calm whenever I can. I think it would be helpful to remember from chapter one about monitoring our thoughts. Far too often, I have lost my sense of a calm before I even knew it. Being aware of what we are thinking is a vital part of the process of maintaining a calm mind.

Principle 4:
Keep a Calm Mind

5

The Plan

A goal without a plan is a wish. (Antoine de Saint-Exupéry)

As I mentioned in the introduction, it is my belief that the single most important behavioral ingredient in making significant life changes is a very specific plan. The plan is the road map; the game plan which guides us in implementing the ideas and philosophies that are instrumental in achieving our goals. As importantly, the plan will assist us in monitoring our progress. Unless we have a systematic approach of monitoring growth, we are merely estimating advancement toward our goal. A specific plan, which helps us regularly evaluate our progress, also serves as a source of motivation. When we precisely measure how much we have progressed and how far we have come, there is an intrinsic motivational factor which promotes further growth.

The first step as we begin to develop our plan it is to set a goal; the change we would like to see, and or the achievements we wish to accomplish in our life. I would suggest there be no ambiguity about the goal. Make it very specific. I would also suggest that you incorporate SMART goals. SMART is an acronym for specific, measurable, attainable, relevant, and timely.

1. **Specific**. What exactly do we want to achieve. The more specific the goal, the greater the chances for success.

56

2. **Measurable**. There must be an exact means of tracking the specific steps which will be used to assist us in achieving our goal.
3. **Attainable**. Decide if the goal is realistic. Set goals high but weigh in all factors necessary to achieve that goal.
4. **Relevant**. The goal must be important enough so that we will be willing to make the sacrifices necessary to pursue that goal.
5. **Timely**. Set a definite timetable when the goal will be achieved.

After you have selected a specific goal, I would then encourage you to determine if it is attainable and relevant. Once you have determined that the goal is realistic, and that you are willing to make the sacrifices necessary to achieve your goal, you should then establish a method to measure progress and finally set a timetable. Whatever the undertaking, beginning a business, an athletic endeavor, improving a relationship, overcoming an irrational fear, or developing a new constructive habit, you must diligently monitor and measure your progress. Coupling your monitoring system with a definite time frame will keep you moving forward in an expedient manner. Without an end date, you are likely to drift aimlessly, and the goal will become a someday thing which rarely comes to fruition. The time frame helps avoid the fatal procrastination trap which is a primary killer of reaching a goal. A definite time frame provides us with a sense of urgency.

The Heart of the Plan

The heart of the plan is to write down the very specific goal and post it where you will see it at least twice daily, once in the morning, and once in the evening. I frequently recommend a bathroom mirror or refrigerator door. The key is it must be in a place you will see it consistently twice a day. I sometimes will put a note under my goal to remind myself as to why this goal is important to me. When making change, it is not uncommon to become momentarily discouraged. Having written down, not only what I want to accomplish, but also why I am pursuing a specific goal serves as an additional source of motivation. I have known people who set a goal to get into better shape. Often, the additional motivation is to stay healthy for a spouse or for their children. Directly under your posted goal are listed the specific steps you will incorporate in order to achieve that goal. You will also need a step sheet with you throughout the day. You can use an iPhone or any electronic device, or you can use paper and pencil, whichever is easier for you. The step sheet will be used daily to monitor how you are doing in following your steps which will assist us in achieving our goal. The final component is the twenty-one-day evaluation sheet to monitor your overall progress. At the end of each day, record your daily totals for your step sheet onto the twenty-one-day evaluation sheet. The posted goal and steps, step sheet plus the twenty-one-day evaluation sheet are the four key components to achieving success in your chosen area. All four components of the plan are strongly recommended. Remember as you begin the process in implementing your plan you are making a full scale commitment, so I believe it is crucial to do everything that is recommended. I sometimes encounter some resistance from students or clients. They often assure me they can make the necessary changes without a particular component of the plan. Many times these individuals have attempted to make changes before but have come up short. It is at this time; I gently remind them what they have been doing hasn't been working. Perhaps we should consciously follow each of the easy to follow instructions for best results.

How many steps you choose may vary depending on the goal you set. Generally, I recommend between three to six steps. Fewer than three may not be enough to provide impetus and provide necessary feedback for change and more than six may be excessively time consuming and thus counterproductive. If you are undecided, a basic guideline is to start with fewer steps and make a concerted effort to commit fully to them.

4 Basic Steps of Goal Planning

1. Write down and post your goal and why it is important to you.
2. Under your goal list the specific steps which will help you achieve your goal.
3. Use the step sheet to record your daily progress.
4. Use the twenty-one-day evaluation sheet to monitor your overall progress.

Relatively simple, anyone can do this. Keep in mind to be fully effective; the key is to use all four components consistently and conscientiously.

I would suggest the steps, like the goal, be as black and white as possible. We have either executed a step, or we have not. Ambiguity is not our friend in achieving a goal and making life changes.

One point I cannot overemphasize is that in implementing your plan; discipline is our greatest ally. Without following the plan with strict adherence to detail, chances of success are unlikely. My guess is you, like many, have tried before to make changes in your life. This time you will not just try, you will do. Using this specific plan, in my opinion is the difference maker. Checking your goal and the steps in the morning and again in the evening is absolutely necessary for success. It provides you with specific feedback how you are progressing which is crucial for your success.

Revisiting our goals and steps throughout the day is encouraged. It is difficult to imagine reminding ourselves of what's important too often. Part of the challenge of setting and achieving goals is that we become sidetracked throughout the day. Often we don't take time to assess what's really important as we go through the day. We need to be aware of our goal, what's important to us, as often as we can.

Starting Point

Since having a disciplined mind is truly the cornerstone to all real change, I generally begin counseling/ coaching sessions with a goal of assisting my clients in increasing mental discipline and controlling their thoughts. It is crucial that we are aware of what our conscious and subconscious mind is telling us. In order to achieve our goals, it is paramount to first develop a strong disciplined mind which will enable us to recognize and control our thoughts. All other goals follow the primary goal of a disciplined mind.

Once we have developed a disciplined mind and begun to control our thoughts, our mind will be positioned to naturally create the habit of acting in a calm, positive, constructive, rational manner, making subsequent changes easier. Below is an example of a plan for developing a strong disciplined mind which will enable us to control our thoughts and actions.

Goal

Develop a Disciplined Mind—Control Thoughts

Reminder Why: If I will not *control* my *thoughts*, I will not be able to *control* or influence anything in my life.

Steps

1. **Every hour, stop and monitor your thoughts**. If you remember to monitor your thoughts for that hour put a + on your step sheet. If later in the day, you realize you forget to check your thoughts for that hour put a - on your step sheet. This first step will help you to get into the habit of thinking what you are thinking about on a regular basis.
2. **Record on step sheet.** Assuming you remembered to monitor your thoughts, place a + if your thoughts were calm, positive, constructive and rational. If your thoughts were anxious, negative, destructive or irrational place a - on your step sheet. If initially your thoughts were anxious, negative, destructive or irrational but within 30 seconds you were able to redirect your thoughts, give yourself a +.

3. **Record reactions onto twenty-one-day evaluation sheet.** At the end of each day count up the +s and -s in each category on your step sheet and record your results onto the twenty-one-day evaluation sheet. Keep track of your progress every day. This is the time element of our SMART goals. Setting an appropriate time frame needs to be long enough to experience changes in our behavior, but not so long that the end point seems out of sight. As you may recall twenty-one days is also the amount of time psychologists suggest it takes to make significant change in our lives. Initially, twenty-one days may seem like a prolonged time frame, but I think you will discover; if you remain disciplined and committed fully to the process, your thoughts, actions, self-talk, feelings, emotions, and habits will rapidly change. Within a short period of time, these new thoughts and habits will begin to serve as a source of encouragement and motivation.

That's the plan. Very simple and easy to understand, but in order to be effective, it must be used religiously. Again, discipline is your greatest ally.

Crucial Notes about the Plan

Please keep in mind, as you begin your plan, progress is your 1st indicator of success. I would suggest you be concerned with the overall trajectory of your journey. If you are showing improvement, however slight, you are heading in the right direction. Without question, there will be the inevitable stumbling blocks and momentary setbacks along the way. Steady progress, and not the unrealistic expectation of perfection, is your best indicator of success. This is why the step sheet and 21-day evaluation sheet are so important. These key components of the plan provide us with a precise measuring system, which is truly the only way to evaluate progress. Without a regimented measuring system in place you are only estimating progress. Without precise data and facts, coupled with a rational mind, our emotions take over and negatively influence our reactions. When making significant life changes, we need to paint a clear picture of what is actually happening. When during a challenging time, or after a less than stellar performance on our part, it is only human nature, to question yourself and your progress. What most of my students discover is, when they revisit their 21-day evaluation sheet, they have had significantly more good days than bad. They are in fact, making steady progress. Remember Chapter 2. Stay Strong. Take the Hits. It is all part of the process. In addition to giving us exacting information, the 21-day evaluation sheet, also sends a clear message to our formerly undisciplined mind that this is the new improved thought process. This is the new normal. Get used to it, because we are not turning back.

"Progress is impossible without change, and those who cannot change their minds cannot change anything." (George Bernard Shaw)

This plan system can be used to change any thoughts or behaviors. Simply identify your goal and the steps necessary to achieve that goal and closely monitor your progress on your step sheet and your twenty-one-day evaluation sheet.

Behavior Techniques

I am going to add a few additional behavioral techniques that may be helpful in assisting you in disciplining your mind and controlling thoughts. I believe these techniques may also be helpful in achieving subsequent goals. Be conscious not to allow yourself to be overcome by techniques. If these techniques work, great; if not, simply stick with the basic plan listed above.

Stop

The first behavioral technique I encourage people to use, and one I have found to be most helpful is whenever I find my thoughts being anxious, negative, destructive, and irrational, I immediately say to myself "stop." It is a quick reminder that I'm heading in the wrong direction. With fifty thousand to sixty thousand random thoughts entering our head daily, it is inevitable some of these thoughts will be counterproductive. For true change to occur, it is incumbent to catch ourselves when these thoughts enter our head and refuse to entertain them. It is surprising how quickly we can change our anxious, negative, destructive, irrational thought process when we recognize these thoughts and absolutely refuse to fixate on them. Keep in mind, it is your choice. You are in control.

Confidant

Another technique I encourage clients to use is to have a confidant with whom we can share our plan. Our confidant helps encourage, motivate, and most importantly helps hold us accountable. It is much harder to quit on a goal when we have not only made a promise to ourselves but also another person whom we trust and respect. Keep in mind the confidant may be providing us with information we don't really want to hear. As a result, a close friend may or may not be the best choice. Sometimes it is easier and safer to have an impartial party such as a counselor, clergy, or life coach. If you do decide to have a friend be your confidant, try not to take their suggestions personally, and make sure you chose someone who will not be afraid to offer input you may not want to hear.

Accept Responsibility

When establishing a plan with a student or client, I tell them, "If you decide not to follow through with the plan, take down both the goals and steps and bring them to me, tear them up in front of me and say I quit." I will not accept, "I can't do this. It's too hard, or I don't have what it takes." I want them to acknowledge that they do possess the power to achieve their goal and take control and responsibility for their life. If they do decide to quit, they are making a conscious decision to do so and acknowledge they have chosen to give up control. This may seem extreme, but what it does is keep individuals from developing a victim mentality, which is a true killer of confidence and success. There is no reason for their failure except for a lack of action and resolve. Remember, when we selected our goal, we established the fact that is was attainable and relevant. All too often I encounter people who want to blame other people, circumstances or events for their failures. If I can help them understand, they are responsible for their lives, and not others, I am providing them with a valuable service. Forcing clients to take full responsibility is invariably a positive because it gives them the realization that they do have the power to make the changes they desire; they quite simply chose not to. This leaves the door open to try again. If we believe we have no control over our life or that somehow we are a victim, there is less hope for change. Playing the victim is an easy out and a shortcut to failure. The other thing I like about this technique is that when forced to admit they are responsible for their failure, individuals will frequently recommit themselves to their original goal rather than accept their own weakness and quit.

Commit

Whether you are setting goals for yourself or being a confidant to someone, I would strongly suggest you not accept half-hearted comments such as: "I'll try," "it would be nice," "I'd like to," or "we'll see how it goes." Rather than making a halfhearted effort, I would suggest you wait for a time where you are fully invested. This must be a top priority.

Do or do not. There is no try. (Yoda)

Dump Negative People

What seems for many to be one of the hardest techniques is to simply remove anxious, negative, destructive, irrational people from our life. Cutting people out of our lives may sound harsh, but we are doing no one a favor by continuing to associate with people who are on a self-destructive path. Sometimes it is impossible to completely avoid negative people such as a coworker or family member. If and when we are forced to encounter anxious, negative, destructive, irrational people, I have found the best technique is to counter each negative statement with a positive. There is no need for confrontation. I simply enter a calm, positive, constructive, rational point of view into the conversation. As a result, these individuals will likely begin to alter their counterproductive conversational style or refrain from such talk altogether, at least in my presence. It is unlikely these people will continue with their counterproductive talk because in their heart, they know their comments are generally negative, counterproductive, and frequently irrational. Also, by in large, these individuals are inherently mentally weak, and when confronted with a calm, positive, constructive, rational person will fold. There is also a chance we may actually help these individuals change their own harmful mental outlook for the better, or they may simply avoid our company altogether. Whatever the outcome, we will be able to move forward unimpeded.

Relax Meditate Pray

To assist us in maintaining a calm mental disposition, necessary for change, I would suggest we develop specific relaxation techniques which can be employed when encountering negative people or a challenging situation. I believe one of the easiest and most effective techniques is to simply take four slow deep breaths. Make a cognizant effort to completely fill your lungs with air and slowly exhale. At the same time, sit or stand as upright as possible with perfectly relaxed posture. If I am standing, I allow my arms to fall totally relaxed form my shoulders either at my side or in front of me. If I am seated, I rest my hands in my lap. I am conscious of tension anywhere in my body and simply let it go. It seems surprising to some that we can maintain ideal posture and keep our muscles perfectly relaxed at the same time. It is an illuminating fact to many that correct posture is more relaxing than slouching. This is partly because proper posture facilitates improved breathing. Optimal posture also allows muscles to work more efficiently so they do not become as easily fatigued. Standing or sitting tall also provides us with a feeling of confidence. An added benefit is that we can use this technique alone or in a crowd. It is rare anyone notices what we are doing. All others see is a calm, confident person who gives every impression of being relaxed and in control.

If alone, and you would prefer, you can close your eyes to enhance relaxation. Some may refer to these relaxation techniques as meditation or prayer. Whatever we call it, ten to fifteen minutes or more twice a day has proved to be highly beneficial in assisting in helping control thoughts and calming the mind and making the changes necessary to developing mental discipline. Personally, I like to begin and end each day by reading positive thinking quotes on the internet. What better way to begin and end the day than with optimistic thoughts.

Smile

On a biochemical level, smiling releases endorphins and serotonin. Endorphins are natural painkillers. The more endorphins our brain releases, the more our body can fight off symptoms of illness. Similarly, serotonin is a brain chemical that acts as a natural antidepressant. It is amazing the impact a smile has on our mental state, and how it can assist us in achieving our goal of developing a calm, strong, disciplined, and rational mind.

Act as If

The Act as If Technique is used when we are not feeling as calm, positive, constructive, and rational as we would like. We are all humans, and there are times when we are not at our best mentally. New situations or unfamiliar settings help create anxiety. We may be in a new job, surrounded by coworkers with whom we are unfamiliar, or about to make an important presentation or speech before a large group. We may be participating in an important athletic event with numerous spectators. Whatever the situation, it is crucial to Act as If we are calm, positive, constructive, and rational. Not only are we trying to convince others of our own confidence and competence, we are trying to convince ourselves too. Whatever the situation, watch your body language. Check your posture, stand or sit tall. Be aware of your facial expressions and gestures. Make your mannerisms welcoming and confident.

When we are nervous, there is a tendency to move quickly and fidget and unknowingly strike a defensive unwelcomingly posture. To counter these mannerisms, move a little slower than usual and think of acting gracefully. This would be an excellent time to practice our breathing techniques. Greet people with a smile and a firm handshake. Prior to any new or anxiety provoking event would be an opportunity to call upon our confidant to help evaluate behaviors and provide us with constructive feedback. Whenever I think of the Act as If Behavioral Techniques, I am reminded of President Franklin Roosevelt, while in the midst of The Great Depression, telling Academy Award Winner actor Orson Welles, "You and I are the greatest actors in America." If it worked for Roosevelt, it will likely work for us. These Act as If behaviors may seem awkward and unnatural at first, but as we muster the behavioral discipline to at least act calm and confident, our thoughts will begin to mirror our actions.

Dress for Success—Get Moving

While I'm not suggesting the need to invest hundreds of dollars in a new wardrobe, I would encourage you to watch your dress and personal hygiene. Sounds rather simplistic, but have you ever noticed that when someone is depressed or going through a difficult time in their life, their personal appearance can rapidly deteriorate? The simple act of showering, shaving, combing one's hair, and putting on fresh clean clothes can have a startlingly positive effect on our mental and emotional well-being. The same can be said for exercise. Much like smiling, exercise releases endorphins which interact with receptors in the brain that reduce our perception of pain (physical or psychological). Endorphins also trigger a positive feeling in the body similar to morphine. Exercise is also considerably cheaper and safer than morphine.

Absurd Analogies

When helping people realize how destructive their thought process has become, I will sometimes resort to using absurd analogies. I may ask them if they would like a delicious plate of lard or perhaps a yummy bowl of mud. Invariably my client or student will look at me as though I have lost my mind and respond "of course not."

I will ask, "Why not?"

And as you might expect, they reply with something along the lines of, "It would taste terrible and make me sick or kill me."

My response is, "Really, so what you are telling me is if you put harmful junk into your body it could cause irreparable damage?" Usually, I just sit back and let that soak in for a minute. Generally, they get the point. What we put into our mind, or allow to stay there can be every bit as destructive as what we put into our bodies. Frequently, people are not fully aware of the dramatically negative affect our thoughts have on our lives.

Visualization

Quite often, it is helpful to create a clear concise picture of what our goal will look like when completed. Sitting for a few minutes each day and visualizing what a completed goal might look like can be time well spent. It not only reminds us of what is important but also serves as a nudge to keep us moving in the right direction with our steps. If the goal is something tangible like a new house, car, or boat, we might put up a picture next to our goals and steps.

I have had athletes whose goal was to win a championship who post pictures of victory ceremonies in their particular sport. Some of my more artistic clients/students will actually draw a picture of what their completed goal looks like. There will likely be times in our effort to make change or reach a goal that we question ourselves. We may be temporarily overwhelmed with the effort needed to accomplish our goal and ask ourselves, "Why am I doing this, why am I working so hard and making these sacrifices?" Having that clear precise visual image of where we are heading may be just the encouragement necessary to keep us on track.

Clearly there are far more behavioral techniques I could have listed. The ones I have presented here have been successful for me and have become some of my go to techniques for clients/students. I would recommend as you begin to develop your plan, you first choose a very specific goal and steps. Use techniques that will assist and not overwhelm or be a distraction. You can always add as you progress.

One Final Note As I stated earlier, for best results in making significant life changes, it is wise to begin with the goal of developing a disciplined mind and controlling our thoughts. Once you have made significant progress in this area you can use the plan to make subsequent changes in other areas of your life. Simply remember to follow the four basic steps.

1. Write down and post your goal and why it's important to you.
2. Under your goals list the specific steps which will help you achieve your goals.
3. Use the step sheet to record daily progress.
4. Use the twenty-one-day evaluation sheet to monitor your over all progress.

Always remember, mental discipline is your best friend and greatest ally. Keep it simple, be disciplined, follow the plan precisely and watch yourself grow.

Daily Step Sheet SAMPLE

Date

Time	Monitored Thoughts Hourly	Reaction to Monitored Area	
7:00	+	+	This sample illustrates how to use the Daily Step Sheet. In the first column, **Monitored Thoughts Hourly**, place a + if you remembered to monitor your thoughts for that hour. If you later realize you forgot to monitor your thoughts for that hour, place a -.
8:00	-	-	In the second column, **Reaction to Monitored Area**, if your thoughts were calm, positive constructive, rational, place a +.
9:00	+	-	Remember, you get 30 seconds to redirect your thoughts if they were initially anxious, negative, destructive, irrational. If your thoughts remain anxious, negative, destructive, irrational, place a -.
10:00	+	-	
11:00	+	+	
12:00	+	+	As you can see in the first column, I remembered to monitor my thoughts 9 times. There were 3 times I forgot to monitor my thoughts in the allotted 12 hour period. In the second column, Reaction to Monitored Area, my thoughts were calm, positive, constructive 6 times and anxious, negative, destructive, irrational 6 times.
1:00	-	-	
2:00	-	-	
3:00	+	-	
4:00	+	+	
5:00	+	+	If I forgot to monitor my thoughts in the first column, I will place a - in the second column as well. As you can see, I tallied my totals under each column.
6:00	+	+	
Tallies	+9 -3	+6 -6	

21-Day Evaluation Sheet SAMPLE

Day	Monitored Thoughts Hourly	Reaction to Monitored Area	
1	+9 -3	+6 -6	After I tallied my monitored thoughts and my reactions to the monitored areas from the Daily Step Sheet, I now record my totals onto the 21-Day Evaluation Sheet. I have used 6 days as an example.
2	+9 -3	+6 -6	As I evaluate the first 6 days, I can see I am improving – not only at monitoring my thoughts, but also in my reaction to events. Assuming this
3	+10 -2	+7 -5	trend continues over the 21-day period, I will almost assuredly develop a disciplined, strong
4	+10 -2	+8 -4	mind. I will be in control of my thoughts and actions. My thoughts and actions will become
5	+12 -0	+8 -4	calmer, more positive, constructive and rational. My self-talk, feelings and emotions, as well as my
6	+12 -0	+9 -3	habits will become an ally I can count on. Feel free to run copies of the Daily Step Sheet and the 21-Day Evaluation Sheet.
7			
8			
9			
10			

Daily Step Sheet

Date:

Time	Monitored Thoughts Hourly	Reaction to Monitored Area
7:00		
8:00		
9:00		
10:00		
11:00		
12:00		
1:00		
2:00		
3:00		
4:00		
5:00		
6:00		
Tallies		

Date:

Time	Monitored Thoughts Hourly	Reaction to Monitored Area
7:00		
8:00		
9:00		
10:00		
11:00		
12:00		
1:00		
2:00		
3:00		
4:00		
5:00		
6:00		
Tallies		

21-Day Evaluation Sheet

Day	Monitored Thoughts Hourly	Reaction to Monitored Area		Day	Monitored Thoughts Hourly	Reaction to Monitored Area
1				11		
2				12		
3				13		
4				14		
5				15		
6				16		
7				17		
8				18		
9				19		
10				20		
				21		

About the Author

Paul Halpine has been a high school teacher, counselor, as well as football coach, and golf instructor for over thirty-five years. Most recently, Paul has begun a new career as a life coach/counselor. Students, clients, and athletes comment that Paul's greatest strengths are in his ability to break down what initially appeared to be complex issues and transform them into more easily understood concepts. One former student commented, "Mr. Halpine creates a relaxed friendly environment and has a way of motivating without being threatening. He really makes you believe in yourself."

Paul is sincere and cares about all his students, athletes and clients. His major goal is to help everyone he encounters achieve at their highest level. Over the years, he has been part of numerous conference, district, and state championships. Several of his athletes have gone on to play Division I College Athletics including eight football players who played for Paul's beloved Nebraska Cornhuskers. Many of his athletes credit not only their physical training and preparation but point to the mental preparation that provided them with the extra edge that allowed them to complete at the highest levels. Paul has been married for forty-five years, has two sons, Pat and Tim and has six grandchildren.

CPSIA information can be obtained
at www.ICGtesting.com
Printed in the USA
LVHW040726261119
638496LV00004B/457/P